THE LUNCH BOX BOOK

JENNIE WALTERS

Illustrated by
Rowan Barnes-Murphy

Hippo

Acknowledgements

Grateful thanks to the following for their help: Jane Brind and the JAPS cookery club, children and staff at Dulwich Hamlet School, Helen Greathead and Sarah Allison at Scholastic Children's Books, Emily and Lucy Phillips, and Miriam Richardson. Plus my family for eating all the mistakes!

CONTENTS

Scholastic Children's Books
Scholastic Publications Ltd,
7-9 Pratt Street, London NW1 OAE, UK

Scholastic Inc.,
730 Broadway, New York, NY 10003, USA

Scholastic Canada Ltd,
123 Newkirk Road, Richmond Hill,
Ontario, Canada L4C 3G5

Ashton Scholastic Pty Ltd,
Private Bag 1, Penrose, Auckland 6,
New Zealand

ISBN 0 590 55197 3

Made and printed by Cox and Wyman, Reading, Berks

10 9 8 7 6 5 4 3 2 1

BOXING CLEVER

"Oh no! Not ham sandwiches and crisps again!"

If this is how you feel when you open your lunch box, don't despair – help is at hand. *The Lunch Box Book* will give you loads of ideas for quick and tasty things you can make yourself. So pick up a pinny, get into the kitchen and have a go at preparing the food *you* like, not the food your lunch box packer/slave/parent thinks you should eat. Once you've tried a few recipes, experiment with some personal touches ... banana pizza, perhaps?

Just remember to be careful when you're cooking. It's easy to have an accident in the kitchen.

1. Always use an oven cloth.

2. Don't reach across hot pans on the stove.

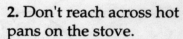

3. Cut on a board away from your fingers.

4. Make sure there's an adult around before you use the cooker, blender or sharp knives.

Read each recipe through carefully before you start to prepare anything. Choose your moment, too. You won't be popular if you start a complicated recipe five minutes before you have to leave for school, or when the head chef in your family is cooking supper. You won't be popular either if you leave the kitchen in a mess.

Another thing to be careful about is food poisoning! <u>Always</u> wash your hands before handling food! Remember too, that warm food should not hang around for too long out of the fridge: cook it, cool it down, then put it in the fridge so that it's quite cold before you take it to school. (A small ice pack in your lunch box is a good idea when the weather is really hot, or use a frozen carton of juice, which will gradually thaw out.)

Your current lunch box slave may well be quite glad of some help with the mind-bogglingly boring task of putting together your lunch box menu five days a week. See if you can score a few brownie points by asking to put your favourite foods on the shopping list. Here are some useful basics you could start with:

- bread mix, white or brown, and pizza mix
- pitta bread (you can freeze this for up to a month)
- croissants (a nice change, and you can freeze them too)
- sweet bread, like raisin bread or brioche
- ready-made pizza bases
- pasta shapes (shells, spirals, space monsters)
- tinned foods (tuna fish, sardines, kidney beans, chickpeas apricots, peaches, pineapple)
- unsalted peanuts
- sesame seeds and sunflower seeds
- dried apricots, apples and raisins
- cream cheese (useful in all kinds of dips and spreads)
- wrapped cheese portions
- peanut butter
- chocolate spread

You'll see some symbols next to the recipes in this book. Here's what they mean:

V suitable for vegetarians

 * quick and easy to make

* * you'll need help and a
       little more time to make this one.

COOKING TERMS

beat stir briskly with a wooden spoon or a whisk.

boil heat until you can see bubbles rising rapidly.

bring together make a mixture stick to itself by squeezing it together with your hands or a spoon.

chop cut into small pieces (about the size of peanuts).

cut into cubes cut into rough squares, by slicing first along and then across.

drain pour through a sieve or colander, so that the solid part of the food stays in the sieve and the liquid collects in a bowl placed underneath. (If the liquid is not needed, drain over the sink.)

fold in combine one mixture with another by cutting and turning over with a metal spoon, using a circular movement to trap as much air as possible.

grease rub a baking tray with fat before cooking, to stop food sticking to it.

grill lay food on a grill pan and place it under a pre-heated grill.

knead make a mixture (usually bread dough) smooth and elastic by repeatedly folding it over and pushing it down and away from you using the heel of your hand, working on a floured surface.

mash break down a solid food, such as cooked potato, by pressing it against the inside of a container with a fork or masher.

rub in use your fingertips to break down a mixture of flour and fat until it looks like breadcrumbs. Lifting your hands above the bowl as you work allows air to get into the mixture and makes the cakes or pastry nice and light.

simmer heat a liquid to the point where you can see a bubble or two rising to the surface.

COPING IN THE KITCHEN QUIZ

Before you start try this little test to see just how prepared you are. (Answers on page 110.)

1. Can you list the following in order of size from the smallest to the largest?
a) tablespoon
b) teaspoon
c) dessertspoon.

2. Do you think a spatula is:
a) a bendy knife to slide into cake tins, or to scrape around a bowl
b) a member of a sixties rock band
c) something you chop vegetables on?

3. If you use a blender you should always remember to:
a) wear earplugs
b) ask an adult to help you
c) liquidise everything first.

4. Do you think a colander is:
a) a helmet to wear on your head
b) a dish with holes in for straining vegetables
c) a type of vegetable?

5. Do you think a masher is:
a) an electric tool for making soups and purées
b) a famous cartoon character
c) a tool with a handle and holes in the bottom that makes great mashed potato?

6. If a pan you are using boils over do you:
a) turn down the heat and blow on it a little
b) run out of the kitchen
c) turn up the heat?

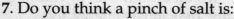

7. Do you think a pinch of salt is:
a) a cooking term for a tablespoon of salt
b) someone who goes around stealing salt cellars
c) the amount of salt you can pick up between your finger and thumb?

8. Do you think a casserole is:
a) a pan you can fry foods in
b) a pot with a lid that cooks food in the oven
c) a type of somersault?

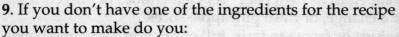

9. If you don't have one of the ingredients for the recipe you want to make do you:
a) not bother to make the recipe
b) try to find something else to put in instead
c) bribe your brother to rush down to the shops?

10. Do you think a grater is:
a) someone who gets on your nerves
b) a metal tool with different-sized holes for shredding cheese, vegetables and maybe even chocolate
c) something you chop vegetables on?

PACK-A-SNACK

These tasty snacks will easily pack into a corner of your lunch box. They're good for you, too!

- **dried apricots and prunes** wonder food! Full of vitamins and iron to keep you healthy; deliciously chewy, too.
- **seeds, nuts and raisins** unsalted peanuts, walnuts or almonds are brilliant with raisins, or you can make up some trail mix if you fancy a lunchtime safari – see the recipe on pages 84-85. A tub of muesli crunch is nice to eat with yoghurt; the recipe on page 84 gives you the basic idea and you can add your own favourite extras.
- **fruit juice** is packed with vitamin C, and helps fight off winter colds and 'flu.
- **fresh fruit** refreshing and easy to pack; it comes already wrapped in its own peel. Try clementines or tangerines for a change, or fresh pineapple slices.
- **yoghurt or fromage frais** full of calcium for strong bones and teeth (page 89 has some yummy yoghurt ideas).
- **raw vegetables** try carrot, cucumber and celery sticks, with dips (see pages 76 - 8) or on their own for crunchy munching. Sliced raw mushrooms are tasty, too.
- **avocados** cut an avocado in half, take out the stone and wrap one half in clingfilm (keep the other half for another day). Pack a separate tub of salad (see pages 34 - 5) to pile into the middle for a real treat.

STICK 'EM UP!

Cocktail stick snacks aren't just for parties. They're quick to put together, and easy to pack in your lunch box. There's no end to the foods you can use! Pack a pot of ketchup or a dip (see pages 76 - 8) and try some of these ideas. Can you come up with some wicked combinations?

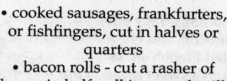

- cooked sausages, frankfurters, or fishfingers, cut in halves or quarters
- bacon rolls - cut a rasher of bacon in half, roll it up and grill for about 10 minutes (can be done the day before)
- cubes of hard cheese
- salami slices, folded into 4
- cherry tomatoes, cut in half, or salad tomato cut in quarters
- pitted olives (the ones with the stones removed)
- squares of tortilla – potato omelette – (see page 62)
- chunks of celery or carrot
- pickled gherkins or pickled cocktail onions
- grapes
- tinned pineapple chunks
- strawberries
- dates
- dried apricots

USE YOUR LOAF

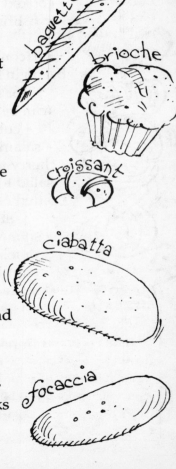

Supermarkets and bakeries sell all kinds of different bread nowadays, so you can do some experimenting. Here are some of the different types you may come across:

French
baguettes (pronounced *bag-etts*) crusty on the outside, and chewy inside, also called French sticks.

brioche (*bree-osh*) a sweet bread, a bit like cake, made with eggs and butter. It's delicious toasted.

croissants (*crah-sants*) flaky dough rolls made with lots of butter but no eggs. These go stale very quickly so try to eat them the same day. See page 18 for some tasty fillings.

Italian
ciabatta (*chee-ah-batta*) a flat bread made with olive oil, it has a chewy crust and a soft inside. Tastes great with traditional Italian fillings like salami, or melted mozarella cheese.

focaccia (*foh-katschia*) a very flat bread made with olive oil. You can split it open carefully and fill with slices of tomato, salami and about a teaspoon more olive oil or French dressing, for an Italian-style sandwich. (This works well with ciabatta too.)

Middle Eastern

pitta bread (*pee-tah*) contains no yeast, so it doesn't rise (it's called "unleavened"). It can be used to scoop up dips like hummus (see page 78), or split and opened to make a pocket that's handy for holding salads and all sorts of tasty fillings (see page 18).

Jewish

bagels (*bay-gells*) round, chewy rolls which look a little bit like doughnuts, without the sugar! A popular bagel filling is cream cheese and smoked salmon with a squeeze of lemon juice. Bagels will go well with almost any filling you can think of, and they keep for several days in a sealed plastic bag.

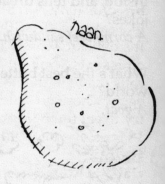

Indian

naan bread (*nah-n*) a flat bread. Some naans are sweet, and some are plain or savoury. Try a plain naan with cold chicken, baked beans or vegeburgers (see page 53).

Did you know?

The Earl of Sandwich was playing cards one day and couldn't be bothered to stop gambling and eat his supper. Instead, he asked his cook to put his meat between two slices of bread and bring it to him at the card table. And so a new convenience food was born. But what on earth were they going to call it?

Some Silly Sandwich Jokes

What's white outside and inside and easily frightened?
A chicken sandwich.

What sort of witches do you find in the desert?
Sandwiches.

What's white outside, pink inside, and tells dreadful jokes?
A corny beef sandwich.

What's the best butter in the world?
A goat.

What's white outside, crunchy brown inside and very slow?
A tortoise sandwich.

What's white outside, pink inside, and talks to itself?
A tongue sandwich.

What's white outside and acts badly?
A ham sandwich.

What sort of sandwich is made backwards?
An Edam cheese sandwich.

SUPER SARNIES

Your lunchtime sandwich need never be the same again! Check out this list, and experiment with some fantastic new flavours, awarding each filling you try marks out of ten. If you fancy a change from the usual couple of slices of bread slapped together, why not make a roll-up, a double decker, a cannonball, or a pitta pocket? The next few pages will tell you how.

Fab Fillings	roll up	double decker	cannonball	pitta pocket
peanut butter, with or without jam	✓	✓		
cream cheese and raisins	✓	✓		
chopped hardboiled egg and sandwich spread	✓	✓		
tuna fish mashed with a fork, sweetcorn and mayonnaise		✓	✓	✓
tinned sardines mashed with a fork, chopped red pepper and tomato ketchup		✓	✓	✓
cooked chicken, peanut butter and yoghurt		✓	✓	✓
salami and tomato slices		✓	✓	✓
grated cheese, chopped celery and mayonnaise		✓	✓	
cold cooked chicken or ham, chopped, with pineapple chunks and mayonnaise			✓	✓
cold sliced sausages mixed with pickle and apple slices tossed in lemon juice			✓	✓
scrambled egg (delicious cold as well as hot) and cooked bacon			✓	✓
cottage cheese with chopped nuts and chopped dates		✓	✓	✓
liver sausage and cucumber			✓	
ham and coleslaw			✓	✓
grilled bacon, sliced crispy lettuce and tomato with mayonnaise.			✓	✓
beefburger or vegeburger (see page 51-3) with salad and yoghurt, mayonnaise or chutney				✓
grated carrot, cubes of cheese and baked beans			✓	✓
Marmite and cottage cheese		✓		

Fab Fillings

You can make a sandwich out of almost anything, so have a
look through the fridge to see what leftovers you can find.
Sometimes, strange combinations taste surprisingly good.
Try some experiments and record the results in this chart:
these ideas might inspire you!

Filling	Yuck	Yum	MARKS OUT OF 10
baked beans and cold fish fingers			
egg mayonnaise and banana			
liver sausage and tinned peaches			
jam, cheese and tomato			

Roll-ups *

Why not try a sausage-shaped sandwich?

You will need

(for 1 sandwich):
    thin, ready-
    sliced bread —
    white or brown

a few slices of
    salami or ham,
    or cold
    sausages

tomato ketchup,
    or one of the
    fillings from
    page 18

1. Cut the crusts off each slice of bread with a knife. Flatten each slice lightly with a rolling pin, so that it is even thinner and will roll up easily.

2. Take the rind off the salami, if there is any. Lay the salami or ham on the bread, tearing off any extra ham with your fingers if it is larger than the slice. Then spread the butter or margarine on top. (This is to keep the bread rolled up.)

3. Roll the bread up into a finger shape, then wrap it tightly in foil or clingfilm and keep in the fridge until you pack it.

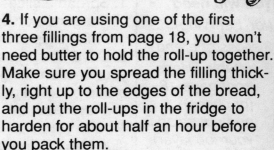

4. If you are using one of the first three fillings from page 18, you won't need butter to hold the roll-up together. Make sure you spread the filling thickly, right up to the edges of the bread, and put the roll-ups in the fridge to harden for about half an hour before you pack them.

5. If you're rolling up a cold sausage, mix a squirt of tomato ketchup with the butter.

Sandwich Sense

Save time in the mornings by making your sandwiches the night before. Store them in the fridge, but be careful not to use cucumber, tomatoes or fruit. These fillings will go soggy and seep into the bread.

You can freeze sandwiches for up to two months, but don't put any salad or fruit in them and don't use mayonnaise or hardboiled egg.

Pitta bread can be kept in the freezer too. When you want to defrost a piece, just put it in the toaster. (Watch your fingers though - it'll be piping hot when it pops up.)

Double Deckers V*

Tickle your taste-buds with some terrifically tall sandwiches!

You will need

(for 1 serving):

3 slices of bread

2 suitable fillings from page 18 (or choose 1 and put salad in your top layer)

1. Spread 2 slices of bread with butter or margarine on one side, and spread the third slice of bread on both sides.
2. Cover the first slice of bread with your chosen filling, then top with the bread buttered on both sides. Spread this layer with the second filling. Finish off with your final slice of bread, butter side down in the usual way.
3. Cut the sandwich into quarters or in half; wrap in foil or clingfilm. Store it in the fridge until you're ready to pack it.

4. If you're really hungry, you could make a triple decker! Use 4 slices of bread, 2 of them buttered on both sides. Cut the sandwich into halves and hold each half together with a cocktail stick. Watch out for the ends when you wrap the sandwich in foil.

Brilliant Butter

Even a plain cheese or ham sandwich can taste exciting if you jazz up the butter a little. Put some butter that's been kept out of the fridge in a bowl and mash it up with a fork until it's nice and soft. Then add any one of the following:

- a squirt of tomato ketchup
- a teaspoon of pickle
- lemon juice and a teaspoon or so of fresh herbs snipped with kitchen scissors (parsley or chives)
- a teaspoon of honey (good on banana sandwiches)

Cannonballs V*

These buns will really bowl you over!

You will need

(for 1 serving):

1 crusty roll

1 of the right fillings from page 18

1. Slice the top off the roll with a knife and set it aside. Pull out the soft bread inside (keep this in the freezer to make breadcrumbs).
2. Pile your chosen filling into the roll and replace the lid. Wrap in foil to stop the cannonball exploding in your lunch box!

Monster Munch

Frighten your friends with a menacing lunch box monster! Take a sharp knife, carefully cut a zig-zag line around the sides and front of a crusty roll, so there's a "hinge" at the back. Pull out a little of the bread inside and pile in your filling. Then make 2 holes on the top of the roll with the point of the knife, and stick in 2 stuffed olives or 2 sultanas for eyes. You could add a tongue made of ham to hang out at the front.

You don't like ordinary bread? Then stuff it! Stuffed pittas can taste terrific. Choose from some of the ideas on page 18 to fill your pitta pocket, or try this tasty combination. (It makes a great salad to pack in a tub, too.) Make your filling first - you can prepare it the day before to save time and put your pitta pocket together in the morning.

Pitta Pockets **

V – veggies - just leave out the bacon

You will need
(for 1 serving):

2 rashers of bacon

half a small can of red kidney beans

1. Carefully grill the bacon till crisp. Let it cool, then snip into pieces with kitchen scissors, over a bowl.
2. Open the can of kidney beans with a can opener and drain off the liquid through a sieve. Add half the beans to the bacon in the bowl, tip the other half

1 large or 2 small tomatoes

2 teaspoons salad oil

1 teaspoon wine vinegar

2 teaspoons tomato ketchup

pitta bread (1 full size or 2 mini pittas)

into a mug, cover and keep in the fridge for another day.

3. Cut the tomatoes into quarters, then cut the quarters across the middle to make 8 pieces from each. Add them to the bacon and beans.

4. Make the dressing in a mug. Measure the oil in first, then the vinegar and lastly the ketchup, mixing them with the teaspoon until smooth. Spoon over the filling in the bowl, then cover the bowl and leave it in the fridge until needed.

5. If you're using a large pitta, cut it in half with a knife and open up the 2 halves with your fingers to make pockets. If using mini pittas, carefully pierce the crust at one point with your knife and slice open one half of the pitta to make a pocket. Spoon in the filling and pour over any dressing in the bottom of the bowl. Pack in foil and take some kitchen paper in case the dressing dribbles!

ROLL UP, ROLL UP!

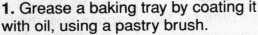

Ready-made bread mix is a wonderful thing to keep in your store cupboard: you can make all sorts of delicious loaves and rolls. Kneading dough is fun, too, especially if you're in a bad mood and want something to punch and pummel! Rolls don't have to be "roll-shaped" – the dough can be modelled into anything you like!

Milk Rolls

You will need

(*for 6 rolls*):

about 1 teaspoon cooking oil

275g (10oz/2½ cups) bread mix

100ml (4 fl oz/ ½ cup) hand-hot water

100ml (4fl oz/ ½ cup) milk

a little flour

about 4 table-spoons milk

1 teaspoon salt

1. Grease a baking tray by coating it with oil, using a pastry brush.

2. Tip the bread mix into the bowl. Pour the hot water into a measuring jug – it should feel nicely warm, not too hot to dip your finger in. Add the milk and stir the liquid into the bread mix with a wooden spoon.

3. When the mixture is too stiff to stir any more, bring it together with your (clean) hands to make a smooth, soft, elastic dough.

4. Sprinkle some flour on a work surface or board and knead the dough for about 5 minutes (see page 9).

5. Cut the dough in half, then cut each half into three pieces to give you 6 balls of dough. Roll them into balls or try the shapes on the next page.

6. Arrange your rolls on the baking tray with plenty of space in between them. Cover the tray with a clean cloth and put it in a warm place (like the airing cupboard or a warm window sill).

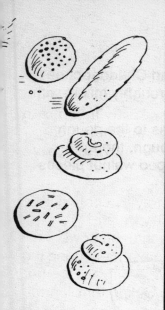

Leave for about 20 minutes, by which time the rolls should have become twice as big. In the meantime, switch the oven on to 220°C (425°F/Gas 7).

7. Mix the milk and salt together in a cup, then brush over the rolls with the pastry brush. This gives them a nice golden colour when they have baked.

8. Put them into the hot oven and bake for 15 - 20 minutes. To test if the rolls are done, take one out using an oven cloth and tap it underneath. If it is done, it will sound hollow. Lift them off the tray with a fish slice and leave them to cool on a wire rack.

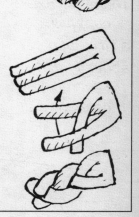

For hedgehogs: snip spines with a pair of kitchen scissors. Fix 2 sultanas securely into the dough for eyes.

For knots: roll the dough into a sausage shape, then tie it in a loose knot.

For plaits: cut each dough ball into 3 and roll each third into a sausage. Pinch the tops of the sausages together and weave them into a short plait. Pinch the bottom ends together too.

Designer Dough

Try making...

Cheesy rolls Add 100g (4oz/1 cup) grated Cheddar cheese to the dough after you've kneaded it and roughly mix in with your hands.

Raisin rolls Mix in 100 (4oz/ ¾ cup) raisins to the dough after kneading. (Don't try to shape this dough, though.)

Walnut rolls Add 110g (4oz/1 cup) chopped walnut pieces to the dough after kneading.

SCRUMMY SCONES

Scones are brilliant instead of bread, and they're dead easy to make. Try the basic recipe for plain scones, then have a go at a few variations. For instance, you can make scones in different shapes, using biscuit cutters, like stars or animals. You can freeze scones, too. Wait till they are cool, then split and butter them, pack them in a plastic bag or a tub and put them in the freezer. Just take one out in the morning and put it in your lunch box – it will have thawed by lunchtime.

Scones

You will need:

(For about 8 - 10)

about 1 teaspoon oil

225g (8oz/2 cups) self-raising flour, plus a little more

¹/₂ teaspoon salt

50g (2oz) butter or margarine

about 3 tablespoons milk

1. Switch the oven on to 200°C (400°F/Gas 6). Grease a baking tray with the oil, using a pastry brush.

2. Sieve 225g of flour into a bowl with the salt. Add the margarine or butter and rub it into the flour with your fingertips until the mixture looks like breadcrumbs (see page 9).

3. Measure the milk into a mug, add the egg and mix them together with a fork. Pour this into the bowl and mix to a soft dough, first with a table knife and then your hands (add a little more milk if it is dry and crumbly).

4. Sprinkle some flour onto a board or work surface. Flatten the dough out with your hands until it is quite level and about 2cm (1in) thick.

(Don't make the dough too thin or you won't be able to split your scones open easily when they're baked.) Stamp out rounds or other shapes with a biscuit cutter or the top of a mug. Use the left-over dough to make the last scones.

5. Using a sieve, lightly dust some flour onto the scones. Arrange them on the greased baking trays.

6. Carefully put the tray into the hot oven and bake the scones for about 15 minutes. Leave them on the tray for 5 minutes or so, then lift them off with a fish slice and cool them on a wire rack.

Savoury ideas

Try making ...

Cheese scones Add 100g (4 oz/1 cup) grated Cheddar cheese, plus 2 tablespoons chopped chives (fresh or dried), or ½ teaspoon dried mustard at stage 3.

Nutty scones Reduce the amount of butter or margarine to 25g (1oz) and rub in 2 tablespoons of crunchy peanut butter after you've mixed in the fat.

Tangy tomato scones Slice a couple of spring onions, and add, with 1 tablespoon of tomato relish, at stage 3.

Sweet ideas

Try making...

Potato scones Add a teaspoon of baking powder and a tablespoon of caster sugar to the flour. Then mix in 125g (4oz/1 cup) cold mashed potato at stage 3.

Fruit scones Add 2 tablespoons caster sugar to the flour and leave out the salt. Mix in 75g (3oz /½ cup) sultanas at stage 3.

Treacle scones Add 2 tablespoons soft brown sugar to the flour. In a measuring jug dissolve 2 tablespoons black treacle in 2 tablespoons hot water. Make up to the 150ml (¼pint/½ cup) mark with milk, and use instead of the egg and milk mixture at stage 4.

Why did the farmer drive across his potato patch with a steam roller?
Because he wanted to grow mashed potatoes.

What do you get if you cross an elephant with some peanut butter?
Peanut butter that never forgets or an elephant that sticks to the roof of your mouth.

WINTER WARMERS

It's chilly outside and sandwiches don't appeal? Well, pack some piping hot soup instead! Make it the day before, to save time in the morning, and take along a homemade roll (pages 24 - 5), a savoury scone (pages 27 - 29), or some crunchy sesame croutons (see below) for a lunch that's daringly different.

Quick Pea Soup V* *
This simple soup tastes really fresh and it's easy to make if you've got a blender. Remember, though, never use a blender without asking first, and get an adult to help you: the blades are very sharp.

You will need

(for 1 large serving):

½ onion

25g (1oz) butter or margarine

200g (6oz) frozen peas

1 vegetable or chicken stock cube

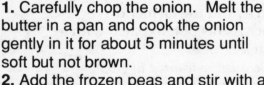

1. Carefully chop the onion. Melt the butter in a pan and cook the onion gently in it for about 5 minutes until soft but not brown.
2. Add the frozen peas and stir with a wooden spoon.
3. Crumble the stock cube in a mug. Boil a kettle and very carefully pour boiling water onto the stock cube, filling the mug. Stir with a teaspoon until the stock cube dissolves.
4. Pour the hot stock onto the peas and onion in the saucepan, then add ¹/₂ mug more of hot water. Cook gently for about 7-10 minutes, with a lid propped over the top of the saucepan so that a little steam can escape.

5. Pour the soup into a blender or food processor and whizz until smooth. Then pour it into a bowl or jug, allow to cool, cover and put in the fridge.
6. In the morning, heat the soup thoroughly. Pour it into your flask, putting the lid on tightly straight away.

Dinner lady, dinner lady, what is this fly in my soup?

Oh, I don't know dear. All flies look the same to me!

Sesame shapes

Crunchy croutons are fun to eat with soup. You can make them in advance and store them for a few days in a tin.

Switch the oven on to 180°C (350°F/Gas8). Butter 2 or 3 slices of bread and cut shapes out of them with biscuit cutters. Dip the shapes, butter side down, in a plate full of sesame seeds. Spread the other side with butter or margarine and press sesame seeds all over. Then arrange the shapes on a baking tray and bake for about 20 minutes. Store them in an airtight tin when they've cooled.

Leek and Potato Soup V**

You will need

(for 1 large
serving):

1 leek

1 medium-sized
potato

25g (1oz) butter or
margarine

1 vegetable or
chicken stock
cube

1 mugful of milk

salt

1. Slice the leek carefully on a board, using the green part as well as the white, but throwing away any tough outer leaves. Cut any large slices in half across the middle, then wash the leek very thoroughly in cold water to get rid of any soil. Now clean the board thoroughly too!

2. Cut the potato into small cubes. Melt the butter or margarine in a saucepan, tip in the leek and potato and cook gently without browning for about 7-10 minutes.

3. Crumble the stock cube in a mug. Boil a kettle and very carefully pour boiling water into the mug, stirring with a teaspoon to dissolve the cube. Add the stock to the vegetables, followed by another half mugful of hot water.

4. Cook, still over a low heat, for another 20 minutes or so, with a lid propped over the top of the pan. (The potato pieces should be very soft.)

5. Add a mugful of milk to the saucepan, then use a potato masher to make a thick soup or whizz it up in the blender for a creamy soup. Cool, cover and put into the fridge.

6. In the morning, stir the soup over a gentle heat until steaming hot. Carefully pour it into your flask and put the lid on tightly straight away.

Hot Box

If your flask has a wide neck, you can squeeze in some even more adventurous hot meals. Try baked beans and frankfurters, or pasta shapes and ready-made sauce, or even leftover stew. Just remember to heat up the food until it's piping hot before you put it into the flask, and ask an adult to help you spoon it in. Pack a long-handled fork or spoon to eat with.

Did you know?
Baked beans were first produced in the UK in 1925. At first they were so expensive that one can cost 9d (which would be about £1.50 today), but they soon became very popular and gradually the price came down. The Heinz factory was called "a protected establishment of national importance" during the Second World War, with its own special guards!

SUPERSONIC SALADS

You'll zoom off to school when your lunch box is packed with a Supersonic Salad! Count down with any of these ideas, or blast off on your own combinations, using almost any foods you can find, cooked or raw. Pack your salad into an empty margarine tub. Dressings need to be packed separately.

Cosmic Coleslaw V *

5. Slice about a quarter of a small white cabbage as thinly as you can on a board with a sharp knife.
4. Add a handful of unsalted peanuts and a handful of raisins.
3. In a mug, mix a tablespoon of yoghurt with 2 tablespoons of mayonnaise.
2. Pour this over the coleslaw and toss with the spoon until it's evenly coated.
1. BLAST OFF!

Oranges in Orbit V *

5. Peel 2 small carrots or 1 large one and grate them into a bowl (mind your fingers).
4. Open a tin of mandarin oranges (canned in juice) and add about 10 segments to the grated carrot, lifting them out carefully with a fork. Add 1 tablespoon of currants.
3. In a mug, mix together 2 teaspoons of salad oil, 1 teaspoon vinegar, ½ teaspoon honey, ¼ teaspoon salt and 2 teaspoons mandarin juice.
2. Pour this over the carrot and orange and toss with a spoon until well mixed.
1. BLAST OFF!

Man on the Moon V *

5. Wash a green-skinned apple, cut it into quarters and remove the core. Chop it into chunks.

4. Add a good squeeze of lemon juice to the apple and toss it with a spoon so that it's evenly coated. (This stops the apple going brown.)

3. Cut a chunk of hard cheese into small cubes and add them to the apple.

2. Add a tablespoon of mayonnaise and toss with a spoon until well mixed.

1. BLAST OFF!

Rocket Raider Rice V *

5. Put about 3 tablespoons of cooked rice into a small bowl.

4. Raid the fridge for chunks of your favourite foods and add them to the rice - try any of these:

cucumber	sweetcorn
tomato	pineapple
red or green	kidney beans
pepper	celery
hard cheese	peas
cooked chicken	sultanas
or ham	
raw carrot	

3. In a mug, mix together 2 teaspoons of salad oil, 2 teaspoons of lemon juice and $1/2$ teaspoon of soy sauce.

2. Add to the salad in the bowl and mix well with a spoon.

1. BLAST OFF!

Some Very Valuable Vegetable Facts

Vegetables can be cheap to buy, but they are very valuable to our bodies. They can be valuable in other ways, too. Read on and find out how...

- Carrots really do help you to see in the dark! They are full of very valuable vitamin A, which develops the eye cells so you can see in dim light.
- The Romans believed they wouldn't catch the plague, or get drunk, if they ate lots of cabbage!
- Watch out – eat too many carrots and your skin might change colour! If you ate nothing but carrots and tomatoes your skin would eventually turn a not-so-valuable shade of orange.
- Before tomatoes were known to be valuable vegetables, many people believed they were poisonous. They come from the same family as the plant Deadly Nightshade.

- The ladies in the court of King Charles I valued carrots so much that they wore carrot ferns in their hair and on their hats, instead of feathers.
- Too much lettuce makes you sleepy – especially home-grown lettuce which has been in the ground too long and turned yellow. It contains a strong drug which is a bit like the powerful drug, opium.

- Cucumbers are not so valuable – they are 96 per cent water.
- Onions and daffodils are related. Rare daffodil and tulip bulbs were very valuable once. They were brought to Great Britain by boat from Holland. One very valuable bulb found its way into a docker's cheese sandwich when he mistook it for a onion. Ooops!

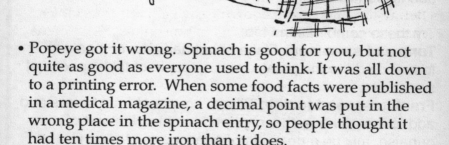

- Popeye got it wrong. Spinach is good for you, but not quite as good as everyone used to think. It was all down to a printing error. When some food facts were published in a medical magazine, a decimal point was put in the wrong place in the spinach entry, so people thought it had ten times more iron than it does.
- The Ancient Egyptians valued the onion very much. They ate an awful lot of them, and believed the onion to be a symbol of perfection, because it was a circle and you can travel round in a circle for ever. They used to put a bunch of onions in a mummy's hand to help the dead person through the afterlife.

SPUD-U-LOVE

You'll often find a little leftover potato in the fridge, and this can be extremely handy for making all kinds of tasty snacks. It's even worth cooking too many to make sure you have some left over to use the next day.

Leftover Boiled Potato

Potato salad For a simple potato salad, just cut the cold, leftover potato into bite-sized cubes. Mix a dressing made of 1 tablespoon of mayonnaise and 1 tablespoon of yoghurt in a mug. Pour it over the potatoes. Chives (snipped up with kitchen scissors) or sliced spring onions are good to add if you have them.

Try these combinations too:

Tuna and sweetcorn Flake about half a tin of tuna with a fork and add to the potato, with a couple of tablespoons of sweetcorn.

Frankfurter and tomato Slice a couple of frankfurters and add to the potato with a chopped tomato. Instead of mayonnaise, mix up a dressing of 1 teaspoon of wine vinegar, 4 teaspoons of salad oil and ½ teaspoon of grainy mustard in a mug. Pour over the salad.

Curried chicken Add slices of cold chicken to the potato and mix ½ teaspoon curry powder with the mayonnaise and yoghurt.

Bean and bacon Add potato cubes to the bean and bacon salad on page 23.

Tortilla (potato omelette) See page 62.

Leftover Baked Potato
Crunchy potato skins Cut the potato in half and scoop out most of the insides. Cut each half into quarters and spread these with butter or margarine. Heat the oven to 200°C (400°C/ Gas 6), arrange the skins on a baking tray and cook them for 15-20 minutes. Keep them in the fridge once they've cooled down, and take some dips to eat them with (see pages 76-78).

Potato skin sandwiches Cut the potato in half and scoop out the insides (keep this to put in another dish). Spread the potato skin "pocket" with butter or margarine and add slices of cheese, ham, chicken or beef, with a dollop of chutney.

Leftover Mashed Potato
Quickie leek and potato soup Slice, wash and cook a leek (see page 32) then add a couple of tablespoons of mashed potato before you add the stock and milk. (You won't need to mash the potato afterwards.)

Potato scones See page 29.

PASTA PRONTO

Pasta is one of the easiest foods to cook, as long as you follow the instructions carefully. Choose your favourite pasta shapes and make them the basis for all kinds of salads. A couple of ideas for recipes are given in this chapter, but there's no end to what you could do!

Tips to avoid a pasta disaster
• Pasta needs to be cooked in a lot of boiling water so the pieces can swirl around without sticking to each other. Use the largest pan you have and make sure the water is boiling before you - carefully - tip the pasta in. (You will see bubbles forming on the top of the water when it has come to the boil.) If the water foams up in the saucepan and looks as though it's going to boil over, just turn down the heat a little.
• Add a teaspoon of salt and a teaspoon of oil to the water before you put in the pasta. The salt is for flavour, and the oil is to make sure the pasta doesn't stick to itself.
• Cook the pasta in an uncovered pan. Stir occasionally.
• Dried pasta takes about 7-10 minutes to cook, fresh pasta only about 4-6 minutes or less (check the packet instructions). To test if the pasta is cooked, fish out a piece with a slotted spoon, let it cool for a moment and then eat it. It should be tender but not too soft. Carefully drain off the water through a colander or sieve over the sink.
• You can make a great salad with cold leftover pasta, but it's better to add the other ingredients and the dressing while the pasta is still warm, if you can.

Tuna Pasta Salad **

You will need *(for 1 serving):*

2 tablespoons pasta shapes

1 teaspoon salt

1 teaspoon oil

1 tablespoon frozen peas

½ small tin of tuna

1 tablespoon sweetcorn

1 small carrot

2 teaspoons oil

1 teaspoon vinegar

1 teaspoon tomato ketchup

½ teaspoon salt

1. Fill the saucepan with water and bring it to the boil (you should be able to see bubbles forming on the surface). Add the salt and oil, then carefully tip in your pasta shapes and boil them as described above.

2. Add the frozen peas to the saucepan 2 minutes before the pasta is cooked. Drain the pasta and peas together through a sieve or colander as described above.

3. Put the cooked pasta and peas into a bowl and add the tuna and sweetcorn. Peel the carrot, then grate it into the bowl (mind you don't scrape your fingers).

4. Mix the oil, vinegar, tomato ketchup and salt together in a mug. Pour this dressing over the salad and toss it well with the spoon. Keep in the fridge until needed.

Instead of oil and vinegar dressing, try mixing together 1 dessertspoon of mayonnaise and 1 dessertspoon of plain yoghurt. It's quick and very tasty.

Frankfurter Pasta Salad * *

You will need

(for 1 serving):

2 tablespoons
pasta shapes

1 teaspoon salt

1 teaspoon oil

2 frankfurters

½ apple (wash the
apple before
you cut it in
half)

1 tablespoon
tinned red kid-
ney beans or
butter beans or
cooked green
beans

1 dessertspoon
mayonnaise

1 dessertspoon
plain yoghurt

1. Cook the pasta shapes as described above, drain and put them in a bowl.
2. If you've got tinned frankfurters, use them straight from the tin, but frank-furters in a packet will need heating up before you eat them cold. So bring some water to the boil in a small saucepan and cook the frankfurters very gently for about 4 minutes. Then carefully drain the water through a colander over the sink and let the frankfurters cool.
3. Slice the frankfurters on the board and add them to the bowl. Cut the core out of the apple, but don't peel it. Chop it into chunks and pour the lemon juice over them, tossing with a tea-spoon so they are coated in juice (this stops the apple going brown). Add the apple chunks to the bowl together with the beans.
4. Mix the mayonnaise and yoghurt together in a mug. Pour this over the salad in the bowl and toss well.

tagliatelle   ravioli   lasagne

Extras

These titbits are tasty in pasta salads:

- cubes of hard cheese
- olives, raisins or sultanas
- grapes
- celery pieces
- walnuts
- spring onion slices
- salami or ham, cut into ribbons
- cooked chicken
- prawns
- sliced raw mushrooms

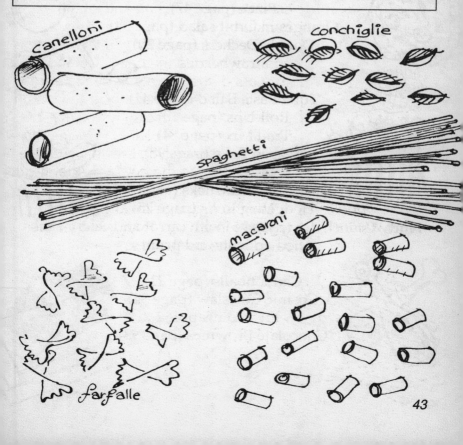

canelloni

conchiglie

spaghetti

macaroni

farfalle

LUNCH BOX PARTY

For a party lunch (or tea) with a difference, pack lunch boxes for your friends and eat picnic-style (on a rug spread out indoors, if the weather's bad). There's no need to supply proper lunch boxes for everyone - empty ice-cream or margarine containers will do, or small cardboard boxes. Label the boxes with your guests' names, tuck in a paper napkin and a party hat, and away you go!

Here are a few ideas for menus:

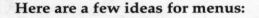

Pizza (page 47)
Oranges in Orbit salad (page 34)
Double Deckers (page 20)
strawberries

Tuna Pasta Salad (page 41)
Roll-Ups (page 19)
Trail Mix (page 84)
Teabag Bake (page 98)

Barbecue Drumsticks (page 58)
Hedgehog Rolls (page 25)
Nutty Crunch dip (page 76) with carrot and celery sticks
dried apricots and prunes

Cannonballs (page 21)
Cosmic Coleslaw (page 34)
Fresh pineapple
Chocolate Brownies (page 93)

Terrific Tortilla (page 61)
Cheese Scones (page 28)
cherry tomatoes
Apricots Bites (page 86)

Pitta Pockets (page 22)
Frankfurter Pasta Salad (page 42)
Fruity Flapjacks (page 103)
apples or oranges

Vegeburgers (page 53) in pitta bread or rolls
Hummus (page 78)
cucumber and carrot sticks
Apple and Apricot Croissants (page 87)

Sausages in their Jackets (page 55)
baked beans in a flask
Potato Scones (page 29)
bananas

Some Lunch Boxes of Long Ago

Lunch boxes aren't a new invention. They've been popular for centuries as a way of carrying food around.

- Long before cars were invented, journeys were often long and difficult. It could take days to reach a place we can now get to in a matter of hours. So travellers needed to take food with them, and packed lunches began.

- In the fields, too, labourers would take a packed lunch with them so they didn't have to waste time rushing home to eat and back again.

- Picnics weren't always eaten outside. Originally, a 'picnic' meant a meal where each guest would bring a course.

- In the early nineteenth century, the phrase 'picnicking and nicknacking' meant that someone was up to no good!

- ...so, when The Picnic Club was set up in 1802, people were very suspicious, and the picknickers acquired a bad reputation. In fact, all the members did was to go to the theatre and eat a picnic supper afterwards!

- The word picnic actually comes from the French *pique-nique* – *piquer* means to pick at and *nique* means something small.

- When the railways were built, and more and more people were able to travel, picnics became much more popular.

- As more people lived and worked in cities, picnics in the country became a popular pastime. Huge parties would travel out to the country, with their lunchboxes. Once a year a factory might close down for the day, and as a special treat, the workers would all be taken for a picnic by the sea or in the country.

PIZZA PERFECTO

Pizzas are great travelling food. You can make them up according to the ingredients you like and have in the fridge, and invent your own specialities.

Back to Base

Traditional Italian pizza dough is made with yeast and rolled out very thinly before baking in a hot oven, but you can make a pizza on all kinds of bases.

Here are a few suggestions:
- Ready-made pizza bases are sold in most supermarkets – the quickest choice. Just brush them with oil before you add the topping. There are lots of topping choices on page 50.
- Use a piece of French or Italian bread, split in half.
- Roll out ready-made puff pastry for a light and flaky pizza.
- Bread mix or pizza dough mix takes a little longer to prepare, but makes a delicious base.
- You can make a quick scone pizza, using the recipe on page 48.

Easy Peazy * *

V - veggies just leave out the ham or sausage

You will need:

For the base

a little oil

100g (4oz/1 cup)
    self-raising
    flour

half a teaspoon
    salt

25g (1oz) butter
    or margarine

3-4 tablespoons
    milk

For the topping

2 tinned tomatoes

1 tablespoon
    tomato puree

1 teaspoon white
    wine vinegar

1 teaspoon sugar

1 teaspoon dried
    mixed herbs
    (try basil or
    oregano)

2 or 3 slices of
    ham, salami or
    cooked
    sausage

1. Switch the oven on to 200°C
(400°F/Gas 6). Grease the baking tray
with a little oil, using a pastry brush.
2. Sift the flour and salt into the large
bowl. Add the butter or margarine and
rub it into the flour with your fingers
until there are no large lumps left.
3. Make a hollow in the middle and
pour in the milk (start with 3 tablespoons first, then add the fourth if you
need to). Mix it all up to a soft dough
with your fingers.
4. Sprinkle a little flour onto your rolling
pin and the work surface and roll this
dough out into a rough circle about 1cm
(half an inch) thick. Drape the dough
loosely over your rolling pin and put it
on the greased baking tray.
5. For the topping, mash the tomatoes
and the purée together in a small bowl
with a fork. Add the herbs, wine vinegar
and sugar.
6. Spread this tomato mixture on the
pizza base, then add the ham, torn into
pieces with your fingers, salami or
sausage. Slice the mushrooms thinly
on a board with a sharp knife and lay
them on top. Grate the cheese onto a
saucer, then sprinkle it over the pizza.
7. Bake the pizza for about 20 minutes,
until the cheese is brown and bubbling

3 or 4 mushrooms

50g (2oz) grated
    Cheddar
    cheese

salt and pepper

and the base looks crisp. Take the tray out of the oven very carefully and cut the pizza into quarters when it has cooled down.

Wizard wheezes
- Freeze pizzas if you have too much to eat in one go. Just wrap the slices loosely in foil and take out one or two the night before for an instant lunch box filler.
- To pack pizzas neatly, put 2 slices on top of each other with the filling in the middle – then you won't have cheese and tomato all over everything.

Tip-top toppings

- If you don't have any tinned tomatoes in the house, you can mix tomato ketchup and tomato purée together, with some dried mixed herbs, if you have them. Sliced fresh tomatoes taste delicious on top of this spread.
- Create an outrageously original pizza by adding your favourite things from this list:

grilled bacon	tinned pineapple
sliced leeks	baked beans
tuna fish	cooked peas
prawns	grated carrot
sweetcorn	sliced spring onions
anchovies	sliced peppers
black olives	sliced spinach
sultanas	onion

- For a real Italian taste, use mozzarella cheese. (It melts into deliciously chewy strands after cooking.) You can try grated Parmesan cheese too, which has a very strong flavour.

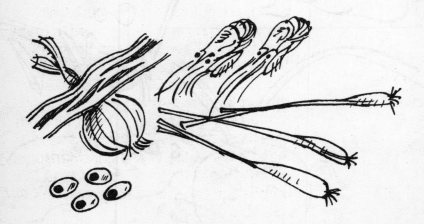

BURGER BAR

Burgers taste great cold as well as hot, especially with lots of extras. Lettuce, cucumber, tomato and cheese are good choices, and you can add all kinds of pickles and relishes. Burgers are easy to make – try out this simple recipe, then the sauce suggestions.

The Basic Burger **

You will need
(for about 4 burgers):

125g (4oz) lean minced beef

2 teaspoons tomato puree

1 clove garlic (if you like it)

½ teaspoon dried mixed herbs

½ teaspoon salt

1. To make your burgers stay together, knead the meat with clean hands. Put the minced beef into a bowl and squash it smooth with your fingers.
2. Add the tomato puree and, if you are using garlic, crush it with a press and put it in the bowl. (If you don't have a garlic press, slice the clove on a board, sprinkle on a little salt and crush it to a paste with the blade of the knife.) Add the mixed herbs and the salt and mix everything in thoroughly with your clean hands.
3. Take handfuls of the mixture, roll them into balls and flatten them to make thin burger shapes. Switch on the grill, and when it has heated up, grill the burgers for about 5 minutes each side, turning them over with a fish slice.
4. When the burgers are cooked, let them cool down, then cover them and keep them in the fridge. Fill a bun with some salad when you're ready to go, add the burger and take some sauce in a separate little tub.

On the side
- **Mustard mayo**
  Make a really tasty burger sauce by mixing together equal quantities of mayonnaise and mild mustard pickle or piccalilli, chopped up small.
- **Mint magic**
  Mix about 3 dessertspoons of plain yoghurt with 1 teaspoon of mint sauce (this is particularly good with vegeburgers - see the recipe on page 53).
- **Try some of these quick ideas:**
  mashed baked beans (from a can)
  mashed chilli beans (from a can)
  sliced spring onion

Or try adding:
  Cosmic Coleslaw - page 34
  Prawn Thousand Island dip - page 77
  Green Swamp Dip - page 77
  Hot Mustard Mayo - page 77

Vegeburgers V **

Whether or not you're a fully fledged veggie, you'll be amazed by these brilliant burgers. They're really easy to make.

You will need
(for 4 burgers):

a knob of butter or margarine

half a 300g (10.6oz) pack of frozen spinach

½ onion

50g (2oz) Cheddar cheese

25g (1oz) ground almonds

25g (1oz) bread-crumbs

a little salt

1 egg

1. Melt a knob of butter or margarine in a small saucepan and add the whole block of spinach. Cook it very gently with the lid on for about 5 minutes to thaw it out. Put half the spinach in a bowl, let it cool, then cover it and keep it in the fridge for another day (you could put it on your pizza, perhaps – see page 47, or in a tortilla – see page 61).

2. Put the rest of the spinach in a sieve and press down with a wooden spoon to drain away all the liquid (it will be very wet). Put it into a bowl.

3. Chop the onion into small pieces on a board, then add it to the spinach. Grate the cheese over the mixture, then add the ground almonds and bread-crumbs and a pinch of salt.

4. Break the egg into a mug, beat it lightly with a fork, then tip it into the mixture. Mix everything up with the wooden spoon.

5. Take spoonfuls of the mixture, roll them into balls then flatten them to make burger shapes. Heat up the grill, then put the burgers on the grill pan and grill for about 5 minutes each side, turning them over with the fish slice.

Did you know?

Most people think that burgers come from America, but in fact they were first made in the middle of the ocean - by Germans who were sailing to begin a new life in America.

Emigrants on board ships of the Hamburg/Amerika line made little beef patties with salted beef from the ships' rations. When they reached dry land, they carried on making hamburgers, with fresh meat instead of dried, and burgers have been eaten all over the world ever since.

GET YOUR HAMBURGERS HERE

SENSATIONAL SAUSAGES

Two quick ideas to make cold sausages even tastier.
Tomatoes go well with them, or you could pack cucumber
slices if you prefer.

Sausages in their Jackets * *

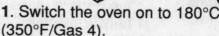

You will need
(per person):

2 slices of bread

about 2 heaped
  teaspoons
  tomato relish,
  mild mustard
  or pickle

a little butter or
  margarine

2 thin (chipolata)
  sausages

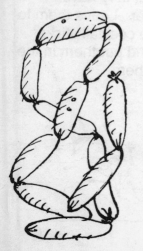

1. Switch the oven on to 180°C
(350°F/Gas 4).

2. Cut the crusts off the bread and flatten each slice lightly with a rolling pin,
so that it's easier to roll up. Spread
each slice with tomato relish, mustard
or pickle (chop up any large chunks of
vegetable in the pickle).

3. Lay a sausage diagonally across
each slice of bread, bring up the corners over the sausage and keep them
in place with a cocktail stick, like this:

4. Put a knob of butter or margarine on
top of each roll and place them on a
baking tray. Carefully put the tray into
the hot oven and bake for about 30
minutes, until the sausage ends are
brown and the bread looks toasted.

Sausage and Bacon Wraps **

You will need

(for 1 person):

*2 rashers of
    bacon*

*2 thin (chipolata)
    sausages*

*some tomato
    relish*

1. Using the kitchen scissors, cut any rinds off the bacon, then spread a little tomato relish on one side of each rasher.

2. Snap each cocktail stick in half. Then wrap the relish side of each rasher of bacon around a sausage and pin the ends in place with the cocktail stick halves, like this:

3. Heat up the grill, then place the sausages on the grill pan and cook them for about 12-15 minutes, turning them very carefully with the tongs about 2 or 3 times until they have browned evenly all over. Leave them to cool, then take out the cocktail sticks, cover the sausages and put them in the fridge until you need them.

How do you make a sausage roll?
Give it a push . .

10 cool ideas for a leftover sausage

- Dunk it in a dip - see page 76
- Slice it up and pop it in a pizza - see pages 47-50
- Roll it up in bread with butter and ketchup or mustard
- Pop it into a pitta pocket - see page 22
- Add it to a Terrific Tortilla - see page 61
- Slice it and heat it with baked beans for a warming winter flask
- Put it in a pasty - see page 72
- Chop it into chunks and add to potato salad - see page 38
- Slip it on a snack stick - see page 13
- Bake it in a scrap of leftover puff pastry with ketchup or pickle

Dinner lady, dinner lady, can I have some undercooked chips, cold beans and a greasy sausage?

Ooh no, dear I couldn't possibly give you anything like that!

Why not? That's what I had yesterday.

SAUCY CHICKEN

You can jazz up plain chicken drumsticks with all kinds of sauces. Why not invent your own special recipe when you've tried these?

Barbecue Drumsticks **

You will need

(for 1 chicken drumstick - just double up the ingredients for 2, and so on):

2 teaspoons honey

2 teaspoons wine or cider vinegar

1 teaspoon tomato purée

1 teaspoon soy sauce

½ teaspoon of salt

1 chicken drumstick

1. Switch the oven on to 200°C (400°F/Gas 6). Line the bottom of a baking dish with a piece of kitchen foil (this will make washing-up much easier).
2. Mix the honey, vinegar, tomato puree, soy sauce and salt together in a mug with a teaspoon. Put the drumstick(s) in the dish and pour over the sauce.
3. Cook for 30-40 minutes in the hot oven. Halfway through the cooking time, take the dish out and turn the drumstick(s) over with kitchen tongs.
4. When cooked, wrap a piece of foil round the ends of the drumstick(s) so it's easier to hold, cover and keep in the fridge until required.

You can also grill chicken drumsticks, which only takes about 15 minutes, but you must be very careful turning them over. Line the grill pan with foil and grill the drumstick(s), turning them over with the tongs so that they cook evenly.

Luigi's Italian Drumsticks **

You will need
(for 1 chicken drumstick):

1 clove garlic

2 teaspoons tomato purée

1 teaspoon wine vinegar

2 teaspoons olive oil

1 teaspoon sugar

$\frac{1}{2}$ teaspoon dried mixed herbs (you can get a mixture called "Italian Seasoning", which is nice)

about $\frac{1}{2}$ teaspoon salt

1 chicken drumstick

1. Switch the oven on to 200°C (400°F/Gas 6). Line a baking dish with a piece of kitchen foil.

2. Using a press if you have one, crush the garlic clove over a mug. Otherwise slice it on a chopping board and crush the slices with the back of your knife and a little bit of salt.

3. Add the tomato purée, vinegar, oil, sugar, herbs and salt. Mix everything up with a teaspoon.

4. Put the drumstick(s) in the dish and pour over the sauce, making sure the meat is well-coated.

5. Carefully put the dish into the hot oven and cook for about 30-45 minutes, turning the drumstick(s) over with kitchen tongs halfway through the cooking time.

6. When cool, wrap a piece of foil around the end of the drumstick(s), so it's easier to hold, cover and keep in the fridge until needed.

Some Cheeky Chicken Jokes

How can you stop a cock from crowing on Sunday morning?

Have him for dinner Saturday night!

What happens when you play table tennis with a bad egg? First it goes ping then it goes POW

Have you ever see a man eating tiger? No, but I've seen a man eating chicken!

Why did the hens stop laying eggs? Because they were tired of working for chicken fe

What made the rooster fall in love with the hen? She egged him on!!

What do you get if you cross a hen with a guitar? A chicken that plays music when you pl

EGGSTRAORDINARY EGGS

Eggs are incredibly versatile. They're used in so many dishes around the world, you probably couldn't begin to count them. They're good for you too, but you must always be sure the eggs you use are fresh. A bad egg can be poisonous.

Terrific Tortilla V **

You will need *(for 2 servings):*

1 small potato

half an onion

2 tablespoons oil - use olive oil if you like the flavour

2 eggs

¼-½ teaspoon salt

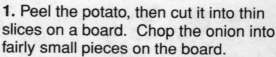

1. Peel the potato, then cut it into thin slices on a board. Chop the onion into fairly small pieces on the board.

2. Heat 1 tablespoon of oil in the frying pan and fry the potato and onion gently until they are soft, stirring them with the wooden spoon. Take the pan off the heat and tip the vegetables onto a plate. Switch the grill on to its highest setting now so it will be ready to finish off the omelette.

3. Beat the eggs with a whisk in a bowl until they are light and frothy. Pour them into the pan with the salt and black pepper, then potato and onion.

4. When the eggs look just set, carefully put the frying pan under the hot grill and cook the omelette for about 4 minutes. Don't cook the omelette for too long, otherwise it will be a bit leathery. The egg should be a little runny in the middle.

5. Take the omelette out of the pan with the fish slice and leave it to cool on the plate. Cut into wedges, cover and put in the fridge until needed.

People all over the world enjoy eating omelettes, cold as well as hot. In Spain, potato omelettes called tortillas are cut into wedges and served with other little nibbles as *tapas*: snacks to eat as you sip your drink. In Japan, very thin omelettes are cooked, then rolled, sliced and served with all kinds of dishes.

You can make a tasty tortilla using leftovers from the fridge. See if you can find any of the following:

cooked potato
carrot
peas
broccoli or leeks
sliced tomato
sweetcorn
sliced mushrooms
sliced peppers
cubes of cheese
cooked, sliced sausages

Other eggy ideas

• Cold scrambled egg is delicious in sandwiches and rolls.

• Plain hardboiled eggs are handy to pack when you're looking for a little extra something to take. Bring eggs to the boil in a saucepan of cold water and simmer them for 10 minutes. Plunge them in a bowl of cold water to stop a dark ring forming round the yolk.

• You can also cut hardboiled eggs in half lengthwise, scoop out the yolks and mash them up with one or more of the following: mayonnaise, sandwich spread, cream cheese, sardines or tuna fish. Pile the stuffing back into the egg whites and stick them together again for easy packing. Wrap the eggs in foil or take them in a tub.

63

The Eggscruciating Egg-timer Eggsamination

Can you answer all 15 questions correctly in the time it takes to boil an egg? (Answers on page 110.)

1. A free-range egg is:
a) one you don't have to pay for
b) one which comes from a factory
c) from a chicken that is allowed to run around the farmyard.

2. Which phrase is correct?
a) the yolk of an egg are white
b) the yolk of an egg is white.

3. The basic ingredients for making a pancake are:
a) eggs, flour and milk
b) eggs, milk and sugar
c) eggs, chips and beans.

4. On which day of the week should you cook your eggs?

5. The shell of an egg is made of:
a) chocolate
b) calcium
c) yolk.

6. What do you get if you cross the white of an egg with gunpowder?

7. Which bird lays the largest egg?
a) the eagle
b) the albatross
c) the ostrich.

Surprise Rolls *

Cream cheese is the base for these yummy rolls - choose your favourite titbits as the surprises. Spread a large slice of ham (not the thin-sliced kind) with a heaped tablespoon of cream cheese, going right up to the edges. Then arrange your ingredients over the cream cheese in strips.
Here are some ideas you can choose from:

- *a little raw carrot, cut into 3 or 4 sticks*
- *cucumber, cut into sticks*
- *3 or 4 strips of red or green pepper*
- *1 teaspoon sweetcorn*
- *$1/2$ pickled onion, cut into slices*
- *1 teaspoon raisins*
- *a few pineapple chunks, cut into slivers*

Roll up the ham and cut it into four sections with a sharp knife. Pack the rolls in a tub so they don't get squashed in your lunchbox.

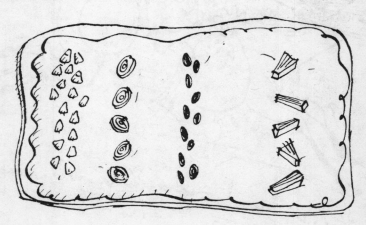

Did you know?

Cheese needs something called rennet to turn the liquid milk into solids. Rennet is found in the lining of a calf or sheep's stomach, and its use was probably discovered by accident. Thousands of years ago travelling tribes would carry milk with them in a bag made from a sheep's stomach. This got shaken around on the journey, and the shaking, together with the heat and the action of the rennet, helped turn the milk into cheese.

You can now buy vegetarian cheese - made without rennet!

PICK A PASTY

Cornwall, in southwest England, is famous for its pasties – flat pies made from pastry wrapped round potatoes, turnips and meat. They were designed specifically as a lunchtime snack, so they're ideal for your lunch box. If you use ready-made shortcrust pastry (plain or wholemeal), pasties are quick to prepare, and you can go to town on the fillings!

A few things you probably never knew about Cornish pasties:

- At one time, tin was mined all over Cornwall and the miners took their lunch in the form of pasties because they were easy to carry.
- Some people say that pasties were made in an oval shape because that made them easy to throw down the mines to the workers below!
- Another idea is that the pastry was joined at the top so that gravy wouldn't spill out into the old Cornish hearth ovens.
- In Leicestershire, people used to make and eat Checky Pigs, a traditional pasty in the shape of a little flat pig, with pastry ears and a long pastry tail.
- Another type of pasty was the Lancashire Foot. This pasty was shaped like (guess what?) a foot, so that it would fit the food tin or the inside jacket pocket of the worker.

Pasties V * *
You will need
(for 4 pasties):

about 1 teaspoon oil

a little flour

1 250g (8oz) pack of shortcrust pastry

1 egg

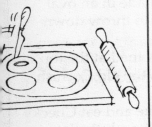

1. Grease the baking tray by spreading over the oil with a pastry brush. Switch the oven on to 200°C (400°F/Gas 6).

2. Sprinkle a little flour over the work surface and the rolling pin and roll the pastry out thinly. Put a plate or saucer onto the pastry, starting right at the edge, and cut round it with a knife to produce 4 circles. (Keep the pastry trimmings for jam tarts).

3. Break the egg into a mug and beat it lightly with a fork. Then brush a little beaten egg all round the edge of each of the pastry circles (this will help the pasty stick together).

4. Spoon your chosen filling (see page 73) onto one half of the circle. Fold the other half over the filling and press the two pastry edges together. Then work around the curved edge with a fork, to seal the edges tightly.

5. Brush more beaten egg over the top of each pasty and put them all on the baking tray. Carefully put the tray into the hot oven and cook the pasties for 15-20 minutes, until they are golden brown. Take them off the tray with a fish slice and let them cool on a plate. If you're not going to eat them straight away, let them cool right down, then cover and put them in the fridge.

Experiment with filling ideas and see which ones you like best. Just remember that cooked meat and fish can be rather dry, so add some "juicy" ingredients like pickle or relish, tomato slices or cream cheese.

Fillings

(quantities make a filling for 1 pasty; increase them as you like.)
Choose from the following:

1. *1 small cooked potato, cut into pieces*
25g (10z) grated Cheddar cheese or 1 slice processed cheese, torn into pieces with your fingers
1 tablespoon frozen peas
1 teaspoon pickle

2. *½ small tin of tuna fish*
1 dessertspoon cream cheese, mixed with 3 teaspoons lemon juice in a mug
a few chives, snipped with scissors, or sliced spring onion tops

3. *1 small cooked potato, cut into pieces*
1 tablespoon baked beans
1 cooked sausage, cut into chunks.

Puff Pasties

You can make sweet fruit pasties using ready-made puff pastry. Roll and cut out the circles as described above, then arrange drained tinned apricots or peaches over one half, or thinly sliced apple. Sprinkle a little sugar over the fruit and over the beaten egg on top of the pasty before

Even more things you didn't know about Cornish pasties!

- Each member of the family would have their initials cut into their own pasty before baking, so everyone knew whose was whose!
- The proper way to eat a pasty was to start from the corner furthest from the initial. Then, if you left it half eaten, everyone could see whose it was!
- Sometimes a whole meal was baked in a pasty - meat and vegetables at one end, jam at the other.
- Cornish people say that the Devil won't come to their county because he knows Cornish women will make anything into a pasty!
- A hundred and fifty years ago, you could buy pasties from a street seller at a penny each.

Some Dangerous Dinner Lady Jokes

Dinner lady, dinner lady, there's a fly in my soup

Don't worry, love, it won't drink much

Dinner lady, dinner lady, there's a dead fly in my soup

Ahh, the hot soup must have killed it!

Dinner lady, dinner lady, there's a cockroach in my soup

That's odd, it's usually a fly.

Dinner lady, dinner lady, this bowl's wet.

Of course it is dear. That's your soup.

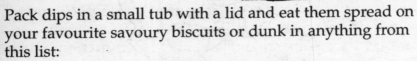

DELICIOUSLY DIPPY

Pack dips in a small tub with a lid and eat them spread on your favourite savoury biscuits or dunk in anything from this list:

raw vegetables, cut into strips
(carrot, celery, cucumber, peppers or
any other favourites)
cooked sausages
slices of cold chicken
corn chips/crisps
cheese straws
bread sticks

Cream Cheese Dips V *

Grab a fork and a small bowl and just mix together the following ingredients for each of these yummy dips.

Tomato Tango
2 tablespoons cream cheese
2 teaspoons tomato relish
½ fresh tomato, chopped into little pieces

Nutty Crunch
2 tablespoons cream cheese
1 tablespoon crunchy peanut butter
2 teaspoons lemon juice

Pineapple Crush
(this is great spread on digestive biscuits)
2 tablespoons cream cheese
1 tablespoon crushed pineapple, canned in juice (or chop up pineapple pieces)

Mayonnaise Dips *

Mayonnaise makes a tasty base for dips of all kinds. In fact you can try mayonnaise as a dip on its own (in Belgium people dip hot chips into it!) but it has quite a strong flavour. Try mixing mayonnaise in the recipes below and see which ones you like.

Prawn Thousand Island

With a fork, mash 2 tablespoons tinned or defrosted prawns in a small bowl. Add 1 teaspoon mayonnaise, 1 teaspoon sandwich spread and $1/2$ teaspoon tomato puree, and mix well with the fork.

Green Swamp Dip

Cut an avocado in half and scoop the flesh into a bowl. Mash it with a fork until smooth, then add 1 tablespoon lemon juice, 1 tablespoon mayonnaise, 1 teaspoon tomato puree and $\frac{1}{4}$ teaspoon of salt.

Hot Mustard Mayo

This one's quite strong, but if you don't want your food to bite back, add as little mustard as you like. You can increase the quantities too, but make sure the ratio of mayonnaise to yoghurt is the same.

  Mix together 2 tablespoons of mayonnaise, 2 tablespoons of plain yoghurt and a teaspoon of grainy French mustard.

Chives Alive

This has a nice strong flavour too. If you like it even stronger, try adding chopped spring onion or raw onion, instead of chives.

  Mix together 2 tablespoons of mayonnaise, 2 tablespoons of plain yoghurt and 1 tablespoon of chopped chives.

Hummus V *

Hummus is traditionally made with a paste called tahini, which contains sesame seeds. It's just as nice with smooth peanut butter, though, which is a lot easier to get hold of!

You'll need to use a blender to make this dip, so make sure you ask first and get some adult help as the blades are very sharp.

You will need:

1 can of chickpeas

1 clove of garlic

2 dessertspoons smooth peanut butter

1 tablespoon oil (olive oil if you have it)

juice of 1 lemon

1. Open the tin of chickpeas and drain the liquid through a sieve into the sink. Put the chickpeas in the blender bowl.
2. Crush the garlic clove in the press, or slice it finely on the board and then crush the slices with the blade of your knife. Add the garlic to the chickpeas.
3. Squeeze the lemon juice into the blender bowl through the sieve (so the pips don't fall in), then add the peanut butter and the oil. Switch on the blender and whizz everything up until the mixture is smooth. If the dip seems a little thick, gradually add some more oil until it is light and creamy.
4. Put the hummus into a bowl, using a spatula to scrape round the blender bowl. Cover and keep in the fridge.

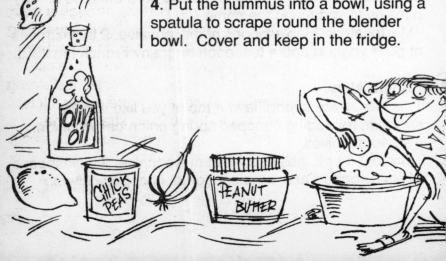

FUNKY FLASKS

Time for a bit of flask action! Whip up a dazzling new drink each day and you'll be the envy of all your friends. Keep it in a jug in the fridge and pour as much as you need into your flask. Remember to screw the top on tightly!

Lurvely Lemonade V **

***You will need** (for 3-4 servings):*

2 lemons (choose unwaxed ones if you can find them in the supermarket)

6 sugar cubes

3 tablespoons extra sugar (soft brown sugar is nice)

1. Wash the lemons well, then rub the sugar cubes hard over them to take off the zest (the outer part of the peel which has a delicious lemony flavour). Put the cubes into a large jug.

2. Cut the lemons in half and squeeze the juice into the jug. Don't worry if the pips go in. Add the lemon halves and the extra sugar, then boil up a kettle and ask for help to very carefully pour 2-3 mugfuls of boiling water into the jug.

3. Stir with a spoon until the sugar dissolves and you can no longer hear it crunching in the jug. Cover and leave to cool.

4. Strain the lemonade through a sieve into the second jug or bowl, squeezing out any liquid that may be left in the lemon halves. Add some more cold water if the lemonade tastes too strong for your liking, and more sugar if it is too sour. If you have strained the lemonade into a bowl, it may be easier to pour it back into the jug for serving.

Chill out

When the weather's hot, fill your lunch box flask about a quarter full with your chosen drink and freeze it overnight (but you can't freeze milkshakes). Top it up in the morning and the drink should stay cold till lunchtime. You can also freeze little cartons of juice which will help your food stay cold as they gradually defrost in your lunch box.

Groovy Juice V *

Make this the day you're going to drink it, if you can.

You will need (for 2-3 servings):

about 10 strawberries

a large handful of cherries

a small orange, peeled

½ lemon

2 teaspoons blackcurrant cordial (such as Ribena)

2 mugfuls apple juice

1. Wash the strawberries, take out the green stalks and slice them on the board. Put them into a large jug.
2. Wash the cherries and carefully flick out the stones with the point of the knife. Cut them in half and add them to the jug. Cut the orange across into slices, then cut the slices in half and add them to the jug.
3. Squeeze the lemon juice into the jug. Add the blackcurrant cordial and top up with apple juice.

Bananachoc Shake V *

You will need
(for 2 serv-
ings):

1 small banana

1½ mugfuls milk

1 tablespoon
drinking
chocolate
powder

50g (2oz) yoghurt

If you have a blender, simply whizz everything up in it until smooth, then pour the milkshake into a jug. If not, mash the banana on a plate with a fork, add it to the milk, drinking chocolate powder and yoghurt in the jug, and whisk by hand.

Sweet Lhassi

Why not have a go at an Indian-style milkshake? They're absolutely delicious and horribly healthy.

You will need:
1 banana

1 small carton
natural yoghurt

1 teaspoon clear
honey

2 drops vanilla
essence

some ice cubes

Pour the yoghurt into a measuring jug, and top it up with water to make ½ pint (250cl). Mix together with a fork or whisk. Put all the ingredients into a blender and whizz until smooth.

Orange Strawberry Shake

You will need *(for 2 servings):*

125g (4oz) straw-
berries

1 small carton
plain yoghurt

1 yoghurt carton-
ful fresh orange
juice

1 tablespoon
honey

2 tablespoons
vanilla ice-
cream

1. Wash the strawberries and pick off the green stalks

2. If you don't have a blender, mash the strawberries on a plate with a fork and tip the strawberry purée and all the other ingredients into the jug, whisking them up until the drink is smooth and frothy.

3. If you do have a blender, simply put all the ingredients into the goblet and whizz them up until smooth and frothy.

Outrageous Orange

For the easiest drink of all, you can forget the flask for a moment - you just need a thin-skinned orange and a straw. Roll, squash and squeeze the orange all over until it feels soft. Carefully make a hole near the top with a sharp knife or a potato peeler, then wrap the orange in tin foil or cling film and pack a straw along with it. When you're ready for a drink, unwrap the orange, stick in the straw, and there you are!

Snowstorm
Give fruit juice a festive touch around Christmas time
with a tablespoon or so of desiccated coconut (looks
good in blackcurrant juice). Take a teaspoon to swirl the
snowflakes around.

What do frogs like best to drink?
Croak-a-cola!

How do you make a lemon drop?
Shake the tree!

How do you get milk from a cat?
Take its saucer away!

What do you get from Nervous cows?
Milk shakes

NICE NIBBLES

A few ideas for some after-lunch treats that are healthy and taste good.

Trail Mix V *

Just take a screw-top jar and fill it with this mixture:
2 handfuls of sultanas, 2 handfuls of unsalted peanuts,
1 handful of hazelnuts, 1 handful of dried banana chips,
1 handful of dried ready-to-eat apricots cut into quarters
and as much shredded coconut as you like (leave this out if
you don't like it or can't get any). Pour some into a small
pot with a lid and pop it in your Lunch Box.

Muesli Crunch V **

Keep this mixture in a large screw-top jar which you can
raid whenever you fancy something to nibble; it's too good
to keep just for breakfast! Making your own blend is fun,
and you can vary the ingredients as you like.

Wash out a small yoghurt pot and use it to measure the
quantities.

You will need

6 pots of basic "no
frills" muesli
(not the
crunchy variety)

1 pot desiccated
coconut

1 pot sunflower
seeds

½ pot sesame
seeds

1. Heat the oven to 130°C (250°F/Gas ½). In a large bowl, mix together the muesli, coconut, and seeds.
2. Measure the sunflower oil and honey into a small saucepan and heat them gently, stirring with a wooden spoon until they are well blended. Take the pan off the heat and add the vanilla essence.
3. Pour this mixture over the muesli in the bowl and stir roughly with the

½ pot sunflower oil

½ pot honey

1 teaspoon vanilla essence

½-1 pot raisins

wooden spoon until it is evenly coated. Spread out on the baking tray and bake for about an hour, turning the clumps over with a fish slice from time to time to make sure they toast evenly.
4. Take the crunch out of the oven and add the raisins (plus any other dried fruit you like). When it has cooled down, store in a large screw-top jar.

Did you know?
The largest cooked dish in the world is roasted camel, which is prepared for Bedouin wedding feasts. Cooked eggs are stuffed into fish, then the fish are stuffed into cooked chickens, the chickens are stuffed into a roasted sheep, and the sheep is stuffed into a whole camel, which is then roasted. Can you imagine what the dinner ladies would say if you took a roasted camel to school for lunch?

Did you know?
Peanuts are really good for you and especially useful if you don't eat meat. They have more body-building protein in them than beef, chicken or fish. You can put peanut butter with all sorts of things in sandwiches, and see page 76 for a quick nutty dip to make.

Apricot Bites V *

These moreish mouthfuls are easy to make if you have a food processor.

You will need:

125g (4oz/1 cup)
ready-to-eat
dried apricots

¹/₂ lemon

5 tablespoons
desiccated
coconut

1. Put the dried apricots into the food processor bowl. Squeeze the lemon juice into the bowl and add 2 tablespoons of the coconut. Whizz everything up together for a couple of minutes.

2. Pour the remaining coconut onto a plate. Take teaspoonfuls of the mixture and roll them into balls between the palms of your (clean) hands, then roll them around in the coconut to coat them. Keep them in the fridge.

Where do baby
apes sleep?
In apricots.

FABULOUS FRUIT

Fruit on its own is probably the best sort of dessert you can eat, but there are loads of different ways to use it.

Apple and Apricot Croissant V **

You will need (for 1 person - increase the quantities for more):

croissant

½ sharp (Granny Smith or Cox's) eating apple, or ½ cooking apple

2 teaspoons apricot jam

1 egg

a little icing sugar

1. Switch the oven on to 180°C (350°F/Gas 4)
2. Peel the apple then slice it down the middle into 2 pieces and take out the core. Slice each half thinly.
3. Cut the croissant in half, like this:

Put the bottom half on the baking tray and arrange the apple slices on it in a fan shape, then spoon over the apricot jam. Put the top layer on the croissant.
4. Break the egg into a mug and beat it lightly with the fork. Brush beaten egg onto the croissant and dust it with a teaspoon of icing sugar, pushed through a sieve.
5. Carefully put the tray into the hot oven and cook the croissant for about 15 minutes. When it has finished cooking, let it cool for a few minutes and then take it off the tray with a fish slice. Keep in an airtight tin for no more than a day or two if you're not going to pack it for lunch today.

Speedy Cheesecake V *

Pack a knife and you can put this clever cheesecake together in a flash.

You will need

(for one person):

2 tablespoons cream cheese

1 teaspoon lemon juice

1 teaspoon caster sugar

fresh fruit (strawberries, cherries, apricots, raspberries, grapes, pineapple, etc.)

2 or 3 digestive biscuits

1. Using the fork, mix the cream cheese with the lemon juice and caster sugar in a small bowl

2. Wash the fruit, slice it if you need to and spoon it into one side of the tub. Spoon the cream cheese into the other side.

3. Pack the biscuits in foil and take them separately. When it's dinner time, just spread the cheese on the biscuits and pop the fruit on top!

Why are bananas never lonely?
Because they hang around in bunches!

Doctor, Doctor, I keep thinking I'm a banana.
Well slip over to my couch and peel off your clothes.

Yummy Yoghurts

If you have a tub with a tight-fitting lid, you can make some great yoghurt desserts. Thick Greek yoghurt is particularly creamy and delicious. Try:

- sliced canned fruit (pineapple or peaches, drained of juice; strawberries, raspberries or grapes are nice) covered with a thick layer of plain yoghurt and then sprinkled with a couple of teaspoons of soft dark brown sugar. The sugar melts into a toffee-flavoured sauce.

- sliced soft fruit, like strawberries, raspberries and cherries (tinned fruit is too juicy), covered with a thick layer of plain yoghurt and sprinkled with demerara sugar. If you keep this in the fridge for (at least) a day, the sugar forms a crunchy layer on top of the yoghurt. (It tastes nice even if it does get jolted around in your lunch box!)

- 1 small banana mashed with a carton of plain yoghurt and a tablespoon of runny honey, topped with grated chocolate and/or chopped nuts (makes 2 portions).

- yoghurt on its own with a spoonful of honey or jam.

- sponge cake and fruit with yoghurt poured over the top makes a trifle with a difference. Try this with ready-made custard too - it's wonderful!

A Few Fascinating Facts About Fruit

If you think fruit is just a little too boring - it's not nearly so naughty as chocolate, or cakes - these facts might help to change your mind.

- A fruit that dates back a very long way is the date! A fresh date doesn't last very long, but it's full of good ness. When it was discovered that a dried date was edible, too, they became a very popular snack for travellers. Maybe this was one of the first lunch box foods?

- Back in the 17th century, many European explorers travelling to Africa and America brought new foods back home with them. Captain Bligh discovered a strange one, called breadfruit. He brought the seeds back to England with him. On the way, he was so concerned about his seeds, that he used the sailors' water rations to keep them alive. Not surprisingly the sailors revolted, and so began the famous Mutiny on the Bounty.

- Sailors often had a hard time in the 17th century. Their ships might be at sea for months without fresh foods coming on board. Many suffered from a disease called scurvy. Eventually, ships started to carry cargoes of limes which were issued to each sailor with his ration of rum. Limes, like oranges, lemons and grapefruit contain vitamin C which prevents scurvy. The use of limes on British ships led to the nickname "limey" which is still sometimes used to describe English people today!
- Did you know that the melon is related to the pumpkin and the cucumber? You can tell if you look carefully, as each has a thin skin, juicy flesh, lots of seeds and a hollow in the middle.
- Do you remember the prickly pear from the film of *The Jungle Book?* It's one of Baloo's favourite foods. It is the fruit of a cactus tree, which grows in Middle Eastern countries. As Baloo's song says, you have to be very careful how you pick prickly pears - they have very long, sharp prickles, which irritate the skin if you touch them. Street vendors who sell them have to wear special gloves to protect their hands.

COSMIC CAKES

Cakes may sound complicated, but these are quite easy to bake. Follow the instructions carefully, and you'll be amazed by what you can do!

In a couple of these recipes, you have to line the cake tin so that you can lift the cake out easily when it's finished baking. Here's how to line a square cake tin. Rub a little margarine or butter over the inside of the tin with a piece of kitchen paper. Then cut off a piece of greaseproof paper about twice the size of the top of the tin, if it's quite deep, or with a border of about 10cm (4 in) all round if it's a shallower dish. Press the paper into the tin and crease along the bottom and the corners with your thumb. Cut down each of the four corner crease marks with a pair of scissors, lifting each corner out of the tin as you do so. Fold the paper neatly around the corners like this:

Trim any spare paper off around the top of the tin, then rub some more margarine or butter over the greaseproof paper lining.

To see if the cake is baked in the middle, carefully slide in a knife: if it comes out with liquid cake mixture on the blade, you know the cake isn't ready. (Put some foil on the top if it is browning too fast, and turn the oven down a little.) If the knife comes out clean, your cake is ready.

Chocolate Brownies V * *

It's important not to overcook brownies - they need to be moist and chewy inside, and they will become firmer after cooling.

You will need:

100g (4oz) butter or margarine, plus a little extra (for greasing the cake tin)

25-40g (1-1½oz) cocoa powder

2 eggs

225g (8oz/1 cup) caster sugar

1 teaspoon vanilla extract

50g (2oz ½ cup) self-raising flour

75g (3oz/ ¾ cup) walnut pieces

50g (2oz/ ½ cup) raisins

1. Switch the oven on to 180°C (350°F/-Gas 4). Grease and line the cake tin (see page 92).

2. Melt the butter or margarine in a small saucepan over a low heat and stir in the cocoa powder with a wooden spoon until smooth. Take the pan off the heat and let the mixture cool.

3. Beat the eggs and the sugar together with a whisk in a bowl until they are light and frothy. Fold in the cocoa mixture with a metal spoon.

4. Stir in the vanilla essence, then sift in the flour through a sieve and fold it in. Chop the walnuts into small pieces, then fold the walnuts and the raisins into the mixture with a metal spoon.

5. Pour the mixture into a 20cm (8in) square cake tin, spreading it into the corners with the back of a spoon. Carefully load the tin into the centre of the oven and bake for 30-35 minutes (test the centre with the blade of a knife to see if it comes out clean).

6. Cool it in the tin for 10 minutes, then cut it into squares, take them out with a fish slice and finish cooling on a wire rack.

Death by Chocolate V * *

Try this delicious topping on your brownies for a special treat. It's soft and can be messy, so pack the iced brownies in a tub and don't take them to school when it's very hot or you'll have sticky chocolate everywhere! The other thing to remember is that the frosting takes a couple of hours to thicken in the fridge, so start it before you make the brownies.

You will need:

50g (2oz/ ¼ cup) sugar

75ml (3 fl oz/ ⅓ cup) evaporated milk

125g (4oz) plain chocolate

25g (1oz) butter

1. Heat the sugar and the milk in a small saucepan over a gentle heat. Stir often with a wooden spoon until the sugar has dissolved and you can no longer hear it crunching on the bottom of the pan.

2. Turn up the heat under the saucepan and bring the milk to the boil (you'll see bubbles forming on the surface). Boil for about 5 minutes without stirring, then take the pan off the heat.

3. Break the chocolate into small pieces and stir it into the hot milk mixture. Add the butter and stir that in too. The heat should be enough to melt the butter and chocolate – keep stirring until the mixture is smooth.

4. Pour the frosting into a bowl and let it cool. Cover it and chill in the fridge for a couple of hours, until it is thick. Then spread it over the brownies *before* you cut them into squares. Keep them in the fridge and the frosting will stay firm.

Rock Cakes V * *

Rock cakes are fun to make, and you can add lots of different extras to vary the flavour.

You will need

(for about 6-8 small cakes):

about 1 teaspoon oil

150g (6oz/1½ cups) self-raising flour

75g (3oz/half a cup) soft brown sugar

75g (3oz/½cup) margarine or butter

75g (3oz/½cup) currants or 75g chocolate chips or 75g chopped glacé cherries and 1 tablespoon desiccated coconut

1 egg

1. Grease the baking tray by spreading over the oil with a pastry brush. Switch the oven on to 190°C (375°F/Gas 5).

2. Put the flour in a bowl and add the sugar, rubbing it with your fingers to break up any lumps there might be. Add the butter or margarine and rub it in with your fingertips until there are no large lumps left.

3. Stir in the currants, chocolate chips, or *glacé* cherries and coconut.

4. Break the egg into a mug and beat it lightly with a fork. Add it to the mixture in the cake bowl and stir with a wooden spoon, until everything is brought together in a stiff dough. (Use your hands if it's easier.)

5. Take dessertspoonfuls of the mixture and place them on the baking tray, shaping them into little mounds with your (clean) fingers.

6. Bake for 15-20 minutes until golden brown. Leave them to cool for a minute or two on the baking tray, then take them off with a fish slice and finish cooling on a wire rack. Wrap the cakes in foil before packing them, or put them in a tub.

Chocolate Sludge V * *

This wicked cake is sometimes called "fridge cake", because you have to leave it to set in the fridge instead of baking it in the oven. Mind you keep your fingers off till it's ready!

You will need:

125g (4oz) butter or margarine (plus a little extra for greasing the cake tin)

175g (6oz) digestive or rich tea biscuits

2 tablespoons cocoa powder

2 tablespoons golden syrup

1 tablespoon sugar

50g (2oz/½cup) chopped nuts

50g (2oz/half a cup) raisins

125g (4oz) plain cooking chocolate

1. Grease an 18cm (7 in) cake tin by rubbing some butter or margarine over it with a piece of kitchen paper.

2. Put the biscuits in the plastic bag and, squeezing out all the air, tie a knot in the open end. Crush the biscuits by pressing them down gently with a rolling pin or milk bottle.

3. Put the butter or margarine, cocoa, golden syrup and sugar into a large pan and stir them with a wooden spoon until they melt and blend together.

4. Take the pan off the heat and tip in the crushed biscuits, the chopped nuts and the raisins. Mix everything up together with the wooden spoon.

5. Put the chocolate mixture into the tin and press it down flat with the back of the wooden spoon. Leave it to cool, then put it in the fridge to set for at least an hour.

6. When the cake has set, begin the chocolate coating. Fill a small saucepan about a third full of water and bring it to the boil (so you can see bubbles forming on the top). Turn the heat down very low.

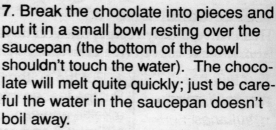

7. Break the chocolate into pieces and put it in a small bowl resting over the saucepan (the bottom of the bowl shouldn't touch the water). The chocolate will melt quite quickly; just be careful the water in the saucepan doesn't boil away.

8. Turn off the heat and take the bowl off the pan with an oven cloth. The next part is a little tricky, so it's best to ask an adult for help.

9. Rest the cake tin very carefully over the pan of hot water for a moment, then put a large plate over the tin and turn the tin and plate upside down. The cake should fall out onto the plate.

10. Pour the melted chocolate over the cake and spread it evenly with a table knife. You can decorate it with pieces of *glacé* cherry, if you like. Cut the cake into pieces when the chocolate has set and wrap portions in foil or greaseproof paper before you pack them. Store the cake in the fridge.

Teabag Bake V * *

This is a very easy recipe, but you have to allow time for the fruit to soak - about five hours, or overnight.

You will need:

225g (8oz/2 cups) sultanas

1 teabag

a little margarine

225g (8oz/2 cups) wholemeal self-raising flour

175g (6oz/½) demerara sugar

2 eggs

1. Put the sultanas into a large bowl. Put the teabag into a measuring jug, boil a kettle and carefully fill the jug up to the 175ml (6fl oz ¾ cup) mark. Let the tea stand for about 5 minutes, then fish out the teabag with a teaspoon and pour the tea over the sultanas. Cover the bowl with a tea towel and let the fruit stand for about 5 hours or overnight, until it is plump and juicy.

2. When you're ready to cook the cake, switch the oven on to 180°C (350°F/Gas 4). Grease and line a 900g (2lb) loaf tin as described on page 92.

3. Tip the flour and sugar into the soaked sultanas and stir with a large metal spoon. Then break the eggs into a small bowl and beat them lightly with a whisk. Stir them into the mixture too.

4. Spoon the mixture into the loaf tin, carefully load it into the oven and cook for about 1 hour. To see if the cake is cooked in the middle, carefully slide in a knife – if it comes out with liquid cake mixture on the blade, you know the cake isn't ready. (Put some foil on the top if it is browning too much, and turn the oven down a little if necessary.) If the blade is clean, the cake is cooked.

5. After removing the cake from the oven, leave it in the tin for 10-15 minutes, then turn it out onto a wire cooling rack and peel off the greaseproof paper. Cool completely, then store in a tin and eat sliced and spread with butter. Pack slices wrapped in foil or greaseproof paper.

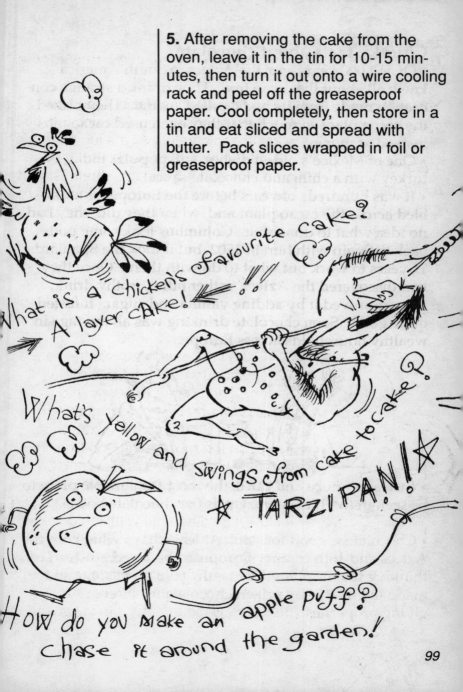

What is a chicken's favourite cake? A layer cake!

What's yellow and swings from cake to cake? ☆ TARZIPAN! ☆

HOW do you make an apple puff? chase it around the garden!

Chunky facts about chocolate

• Over 2,000 years ago, the Aztecs in South America knew all about the cacao tree. They drank a strange concoction made from its pods, called *xocatyl*. They prized the cocoa plant so much that they even used cacao nibs instead of money.

• One of Mexico's oldest dishes, still popular today, is turkey with a chilli and chocolate sauce!

• It was hundreds of years before the Europeans stumbled across the cacao plant and, when they did, they had no idea what to do with it. Columbus took some pods back to Spain with him in 1502, but it took the Spaniards 17 years to work out what to do with them. Once they had discovered the Aztecs' rather bitter, frothy drink, they improved it by adding vanilla and sugar. It tasted quite good! Soon chocolate drinking was all the rage in wealthy households across Europe.

• Instead of pubs and cafés, the most fashionable place to be seen in the 17th century was the chocolate house.

• Chocolate is good for you! At least that's what both the Aztecs and 16th century Europeans believed. Instead of thinking that it rotted their teeth, gave them spots and made them fat, they prized chocolate for its energy-giving properties.

• It took a further 300 years before the Europeans realised they could *eat* chocolate as well as drink it. In the nineteenth century, manufacturers experimented by adding a variety of ingredients. With the addition of condensed milk, *Nestlé* was able to launch the first ever milk chocolate bar in 1875.

• The first *filled* chocolate bar was on the market in 1866. Over 100 years later we're still eating Fry's Chocolate cream!

• The Hershey Bar is famous all over America. It was introduced to the American public in 1894. It became so popular that there's now a chocolate theme park in the town where it's produced!

• The Mars Bar is getting on a bit too! It first arrived in 1932 and was so successful, it's estimated that Mars now produce over 2 million bars every day!

BRILLIANT BISCUITS

Biscuits in a packet can be pretty tempting, but they're never quite as good as the real – homemade – thing.

Peanut and Raisin Cookies V * *

You will need

(makes about 10 cookies):

50g (2oz) soft margarine (plus extra for greasing the baking tray)

75g (3oz/ ½ cup) caster sugar

1 egg

75g (3oz/ ¾ cup) self-raising flour

2 tablespoons crunchy peanut butter

75g (3oz/ ½ cup) raisins

75g (3oz/ ½ cup) unsalted peanuts

1. Switch the oven on to 180°C (350°F/Gas 4). Grease a baking tray by rubbing over some margarine with a piece of kitchen paper.

2. Put all the ingredients, except for the raisins and the peanuts, into a large bowl and beat them well with a wooden spoon until they are mixed together. Stir in the raisins.

3. Put spoonfuls of the mixture onto the baking tray, spacing them well apart as they will spread out while baking. Flatten the spoonfuls with a fork and press a few peanuts evenly over the top of each of the biscuits. Make a pattern on each one if you like.

4. Put the tray into the oven. Bake for 10 - 15 minutes, until the biscuits are golden-brown around the edges.

5. Take the tray out of the oven and let the biscuits harden on it for a few minutes. Then lift them off with a fish slice and let them cool completely on a wire rack. Store them in a tin, and pack them in your lunch box in foil or a tub, so they don't get crushed.

Fruity Flapjacks   V * *

You can make these flapjacks without the dried fruit, if you don't happen to have any in the cupboard.

You will need

(for 12 flapjacks):

125g (4oz/ ¼ cup) demerara sugar

125g (4oz) butter or margarine (plus extra for greasing the cake tin)

2 tablespoons golden syrup

175g (6oz/2 cups) porridge oats

2 tablespoons desiccated coconut

50g (2oz) dried apricots

50g (2oz) dried apple

1. Switch the oven on to 150°C (300°F/Gas 2). Grease a 20cm (8in) square cake tin by rubbing over some butter or margarine with a piece of kitchen paper.

2. Melt the sugar, butter or margarine, and golden syrup in a large saucepan over a gentle heat, stirring from time to time with a wooden spoon.

3. Take the saucepan off the heat and stir in the porridge oats and coconut, mixing everything together with the wooden spoon. Snip the dried apricots and apple into pieces with scissors and add them to the saucepan too.

4. Put the mixture into the cake tin and press it down evenly with your (clean) fingers. Bake for about 35 minutes, then take out the tin, let the flapjacks cool for about 10 minutes and mark them into about 12 bars with a knife. Leave them to cool a little. When you can easily touch the warm tin, tip the flapjacks onto a cooling rack.

Fruit Slices V * *

These slices tend to be rather crumbly, so wrap them in foil before you pack them.

You will need

(for about 12):

125g (4oz) ready-to-eat dried apricots

125g (4oz) ready-to-eat dried prunes

125g (4oz) chopped dates

150ml (6 fl oz/¾ cup) water

150g (5oz) butter or margarine (plus extra for greasing the cake tin)

75g (3oz/½ cup) soft brown or demerara sugar

225g (8oz/2 cups) wholemeal flour

100g (4oz) porridge oats

1. Switch the oven on to 200°C (400°F/Gas 6). Then grease a 28 x 18cm (11 x 7in) cake tin by rubbing over some butter or margarine with a piece of kitchen paper.

2. Snip the apricots and prunes into pieces with the kitchen scissors over a medium-sized saucepan. Add the dates, then pour in the water and cook over a gentle heat until the fruit is soft (about 15 minutes).

3. Melt the butter or margarine and sugar in a large saucepan over a gentle heat, stirring from time to time with a wooden spoon. Then take the pan off the heat and tip in the flour and porridge oats little by little, stirring well each time.

4. When everything is well blended, put about half the mixture into the tin, pressing down well with the palm of your (clean) hand so that the mixture is flat and evenly spread out.

5. Spread the cooked fruit over the oaty layer, then sprinkle on the second half of the oat mixture and press it down well with your hand again.

6. Carefully place the tin in the oven and bake for about 20 minutes, until golden brown. Take the tin out of the oven and cut into slices with a sharp knife. When they are quite cold, take them out with a fish slice, and store in an airtight tin.

Did you hear about the fight in the biscuit tin?
A Bandit hit a Penguin with a Club, tied it up with a Blue Ribband and got away in a Taxi.

What's brown, prickly and squirts jam at you?
A hedgehog eating a doughnut.

What's the best thing to put in your biscuits?
Your teeth.

SWEET SANDWICHES

Sandwiches don't have to be savoury – sweet, fruity ones are delicious too. If you don't have any sweet bread to hand, try plain brown bread (see pages 14-15 for more information). It's best to make these the morning you need them, but they are very quick.

Tutti Frutti

You will need

(for 1 serving):

2 slices of sweet bread, such as raisin bread or brioche

about 2 table-spoons of cream cheese or chocolate spread

fresh sliced fruit, such as grapes, strawberries, bananas, nectarines, etc.

Spread both slices of the bread with cream cheese. Pile the fruit on top of one slice and top with the second, spread side down.

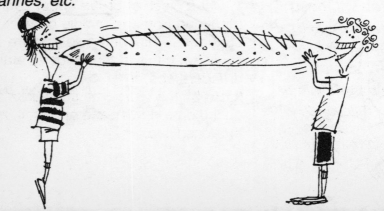

Sandwich Suggestions

Why not have a go inventing your own sweet sandwiches?
Choose a bread base, then your own combination of
wicked fillings:

bread base	**filling**
croissants	banana
bagels	brown sugar
waffles	jam
cream crackers	cream cheese
malt bread	lemon curd
walnut bread	golden syrup
(pack waffles and	condensed milk
cream crackers	marmalade
with a knife, spread	sultanas
on your	
filling at lunchtime)	

Channel Tunnel

Children in France love chocolate sandwiches. It sounds a
bit strange, but once you've tried them you'll be hooked.

You will need

(for 1 serving):

*a French stick
(baguette)*

*a bar of plain or
milk chocolate
(whichever is
your favourite)*

1. Cut a piece of bread about 20cm
(8in) long from the middle of the
baguette. Pull out the soft centre (you
could keep this in the fridge to make
breadcrumbs).
2. Break the chocolate into sticks and
push some down each end until the
bread is filled.

A QUICK QUIZ

Now you've read the book from cover to cover, can you answer all 10 questions correctly, and prove you've digested every word?...(The Answers are on page 110.)

1. Pasta is mainly eaten in:
a) Italy
b) China
c) restaurants.

2. A croissant is:
a) a long French loaf
b) a flaky roll made from eggs and butter
c) a type of fruit.

3. Can you match the type of bread to the country it comes from?
a) naan   1) Italy
b) ciabatta   2) India
c) pitta   3) France
d) brioche   4) Middle East

4. Which of these tasty sandwiches shouldn't be frozen?
a) bacon and chutney
b) jam and coleslaw
c) baked bean and fish fingers.

5. A tortilla is:
a) a type of pasta
b) something you wear on your head
c) a Spanish omelette.

6. Which cheese originally comes from which country?

a) Feta	1) France
b) Gruyére	2) Greece
c) Brie	3) Great Britain
d) Cheddar	4) Switzerland

7. The seeds of which fruit caused a mutiny?
a) a pineapple
b) a raspberry
c) a breadfruit.

8. Chocolate originally comes from:
a) Switzerland
b) Spain
c) Mexico.

9. People used to think that the tomato was:
a) delicious
b) explosive
c) poisonous.

10. The word picnic means:
a) food that had been stolen
b) small items of food you can pick at
c) food to eat at the theatre.

ANSWERS

Coping in the Kitchen Quiz (pages 10-11)

1. teaspoon; dessertspoon; tablespoon.
2. a)   3. b)   4. b)   5. c)   6. a)
7. c)   8. b)   9. b)   10. b)

The Eggscruciating Egg-timer Eggsamination (pages 64-65)

1. c)   2. Neither,the yolk of an egg is yellow!
3. a)   4. Fry-day!   5. b)   6. Boom-meringue.
7. c)   8. Terri-fried.   9. b)   10. a)
11. A hen-cyclopaedia.   12. b)   13. Chick to chick.
14. c)   15. One, because after that it's not empty.

A Quick Quiz (pages 108-9)

1. a)   2. b)   3. naan: India, ciabatta: Italy, pitta: Middle East, brioche: France
4. b)   5. c)   6. Feta: Greece, Gruyére: Switzerland, Brie: France, Cheddar: Great Britain
7. c)   8. c)   9. c)   10. b)

INDEX